"Blessed is he who reads this book
and believes what is written, for
the healing power of God shall
be released unto you".
(Harry Walther, Oct 2010).

THE SON OF GOD, The Clone of God

SOLVING THE MYSTERY Of THE TRINITY

HARRY WALTHER

iUniverse, Inc.
New York   Bloomington

THE SON OF GOD, The Clone of God
SOLVING THE MYSTERY OF "THE TRINITY"

iUniverse books may be ordered through booksellers or by contacting:

iUniverse
1663 Liberty Drive
Bloomington, IN 47403
www.iuniverse.com
1-800-Authors (1-800-288-4677)

ISBN: 978-1-4502-6793-9 (sc)
ISBN: 978-1-4502-6794-6 (ebk)

Printed in the United States of America

iUniverse rev. date: 10/28/2010

Now, in light of major scientific
Breakthroughs in Genetics, we
Can finally under the "Trinity"
And who The Bible declares
JESUS to be in a clear
And tangible way.

Table of Contents

INTRODUCTION 1

ONE: MESSIAH IN OLD TESTAMENT 3

TWO: JESUS – SON OF GOD 7

THREE: TRINITY OR BURN 13

FOUR: PROBLEMS WITH THE TRINITY 17

FIVE: THE CLONE OF GOD 22

SIX: ORIGIN IS THE KEY 31

SEVEN: THE NAME OF GOD 42

EIGHT: APOCALYPSE 2012 62

NINE: FINAL CHURCH – TRUE CHURCH 65

TEN: TWO PATHS: CHOOSE LIFE:
THE APOSTLES CREED 73

INTRODUCTION

M any say it is impossible to understand The "Trinity", to solve the Mystery of The Triune God. I say that we can because JESUS said we can for, "With God all things are possible".

I view solving the Mystery of The Trinity like the medieval legend of The Sword of Excalibur. As the story went, the magician Merlin placed a sword in a stone and whoever could draw the sword from the stone would be King of all England. Well many a man tried and failed and then a young stable boy named Arthur gave it a try and the sword magically was withdrawn from the stone and Arthur went onto become King of Britain. We must admit that all of the theologians and scholars throughout the ages and all of the scholars and theologians and famous Christian Teachers today have all failed to "draw the sword from the stone" = to solve The Mystery of the Trinity.

Do I wish to become King of Christianity, or a national leader? Not at all. I just hope this revelation of who JESUS truly is will cause Christendom to open their minds to the new and other "revelations" I have presented since 1986. This includes Two Rapture Events vs one Rapture and the Antichrist coming as a spiritual messiah and teacher vs the everlasting myth of Antichrist as a western politician who has all of the answers.

It is now 2010 and Who JESUS is, and what the phrase, "Son of God" means, has been a mystery and a controversy for almost the last 2000 years. Now its time to learn the amazing truth of exactly who The Bible declares JESUS to be.

CHAPTER ONE:
MESSIAH IN THE OLD
TESTAMENT

There are certain key verses in the Old Testament that state the Messiah (Christ) would be GOD INCARNATE, GOD in the flesh. The first more mystical and cryptic verse is in Genesis where as YHWH GOD said,

"Let us make man in our
own image and in our
own likeness".

Who is YHWH GOD talking to? A mirror? It is believed that GOD is speaking to his Son = the Messiah, who co-created all things with His Father.

Genesis 3 is another verse of the Messiah, that is shrouded in mystery, Where as God said to satan, the devil concerning the coming of God's Messiah (Christ),

"And I will put war between you
and the woman, and between
your seed and his Seed, and
you shall bruise his heel and
he shall crush your head."
Gen:3:15

It is believed by virtually all Christian Scholars, looking back at the Old Testament from a Post- Gospel view, that the woman represents Eve and later MARY who would give birth to the Messiah. He would be killed by men (inspired by Satan), rise from the dead and then crush or shatter Satan's power to those who believe –in (accept and follow) The Messiah (Christ in English). The "seed" being spiritual, for those who are born of God through the Holy Spirit and I accept this interpretation of Gen:3:15.

Next we come to the Book of Isaiah and two more verses about the coming Messiah that are much more clear.

"Behold, a virgin shall bear a
child, and shall call His Name
Emmanuel, which means "God
With us". (Isa:7:14)

This verse is very clear that The Messiah would be born of a virgin and a reference to Gen:3:15 of the coming Messiah and that the Messiah (Christ) would be GOD INCARNATE, GOD or Divinity in The Flesh, with us. This MESSIAH = EMMAMUEL = GOD INCARNATE = GOD WITH US" theme is expanded upon in ISA:9:6

6) "For unto us a Child is born,
unto us a son is given, And
the government shall be upon
his shoulders and His Name
shall be called, Wonderful,
Counselor, Mighty God,
Everlasting Father, Prince
Of Peace".

7) And of the increase of his
government and peace, shall
have no end."

Isa:9:6 is crystal clear that Messiah = EMMANUEL is truly GOD INCARNATE, GOD WITH US, "Everlasting Father, Mighty God, Prince of Peace.

Next follows a host of Old Testament verses through all of The Books of The Prophets that speak of Messiah (Christ) or Emmanuel coming to bring Judgment upon the earth (to the wicked, those who do evil) and that HE will set up his divine kingdom upon earth. Another clear verse that Messiah = DIVINE = GOD INCARNATE is in found Micah, another prophet in the Old Testament,

"But you Bethlehem (Ephrathah), though
you are little among the thousands of
Judah, Yet out of you shall come forth
To Me, The One to be Ruler in Israel,
Whose goings are from of old,
From everlasting." Mic:5:2.

The Messiah (Christ) would be of old, whose goings forth are from everlasting, from eternity backwards `= GOD INCARNATE. (A Prophecy Fulfilled) Jesus was born in a manger in the small Hebrew town of Bethlehem which has been the theme of Christmas and the Birth of Messiah= the Virgin Birth ever since."

Now with this Old Testament, Messiah = GOD INCARNATE theme, enter JESUS and The Gospels.

CHAPTER TWO:
JESUS – SON OF GOD

———

JESUS began his Ministry in about 30 AD and His Words were followed by a flood of signs, wonders and miracles. People were healed of all manner of disease, demons were cast out, JESUS healed the blind and the crippled and the deaf, He raised Lazarus from the dead, turned water into wine, calmed the storm with A Word and ultimately rose from the dead Himself on the third day.

Added to the miraculous, There were certain key statements that JESUS made that caused his followers to believe he was this Hebrew Messiah, "Emmanuel", GOD WITH US (God Incarnate).

In John: 8:56, JESUS had a confrontation with the religious leaders of his day and they asked him, who do you claim to be? Are you greater than our Father,

Abraham and the prophets? JESUS replied, "Your Father Abraham, rejoiced to see my day (appearance) and he saw it and was glad."

In this statement, JESUS was claiming to be the mysterious "Melchizedek, King of Salem and the priest of "EL ELYOM", THE GOD MOST HIGH" who came to Abraham at a time of great danger. Melchizedek gave Abraham "bread and wine" and blessed him, saying, "Blessed be Abram of God Most High Possessor of heaven and earth, and blessed be God Most High, who has delivered your enemies into your hand." (Gen:14:19).

The religious leaders (Pharisees) knew Jesus was claiming to be Melchizedek but were perplexed and said, "You are not even fifty year old and you had seen Abraham? (who had been dead for almost 2000 years).

Jesus replied, "Most Assuredly I say unto You, before was, I AM". (Jn:8:58).

Here JESUS declared himself as GOD INCARNATE, EMMANUEL, as he quotes who GOD told Moses as HE was," I AM THAT I AM "… the ever present one, GOD HIMSELF.

The Pharisees knew exactly what JESUS was saying yet not understanding that The Messiah (Christ) would be

GOD INCARNATE and that he would come as a Man to die for the sins of the world (ISA:53), they took up stones to stone him for blasphemy.

This statement by JESUS as The "I AM" is why John believed JESUS WAS GOD and wrote in this at start of His Gospel,

"In The Beginning was The Word
(Logos) and the Word was with
God and the word was God."
(Jn:1:1).

In Jn:14:9 JESUS told his Disciples who asked to see The Father (God) JESUS said, "If you have seen me you have seen the Father". Again a reference to Isa:7;14 and Isa:9:6 where Messiah = GOD INCARNATE = EMMANUEL.

In Acts, Peter believed and proclaimed,

"Be baptized in the name of JESUS
for the forgiveness of sins and
you shall receive the Gift of
the Holy Spirit". (ACTS:2:38).

and, "For God raised JESUS from the dead and has made him both LORD and Christ.

Christ is English name for "Christo" (Greek) = Messiah in Hebrew. LORD is the Hebrew word for GOD – ADONAI- LORD, YHWH = GOD, JESUS AS GOD INCARNATE = EMMANUEL.

And so… the early church believed that JESUS WAS LORD (Adonai) GOD INCARNATE and believers in JESUS as Messiah- Emmanuel were baptized in His name.

In 70 AD, the Jews and the First Church in Jerusalem were driven from Israel by the Roman Army in the Dispersia and Christianity then developed and expanded in the pagan, Greco-Roman world. Both pagan cultures had many "trinities" and pantheons of Gods, yet their gods were male and female and mated to give birth to younger gods, divine sons and daughters.

From about 150 – 250 AD, the vast majority of Christians believed that JESUS was GOD and a modified version of the "pagan" TRINITY emerged, The Christian God as a "triune" God, GOD THE FATHER, GOD THE SON, GOD THE SPIRIT, THREE AS ONE.

No doubt the age old "Trinity" analogies were started such as GOD as THE EGG = Three parts as a Whole = Yolk- White and Shell. Also The "Trinity" as water as having three states = VAPOR- LIQUID- ICE yet all being water.

At this same time, a minority movement was started by a bishop named ARIUS who claimed that JESUS was not God but something less, a created yet divine being. There were five major Bible Verses (in The Gospels) that fueled the Arius Movement.

(1) A young ruler called Jesus "good teacher" and JESUS replied, "There is none good but One who is GOD, and if you want to enter into eternal life, keep his commandments". (Matt:19:17).

This suggests that JESUS was not GOD but His Son as he stated many times in The Gospels.

(2) JOHN:3:16, "For God so loved the world that He Gave His "Only-begotten Son". "Only Begotten Son" seemed to suggest that Jesus was born or "brought into existence.

(3) Dying upon the cross where as JESUS cried out, "My God, My God, why have you forsaken me?" (the question is "How can God forsake God?).

(4) Jesus saying to Mary Magdalene, After His Resurrection, "Do not touch (hold) me for I have yet to ascend to My God and to your God".

How can JESUS as GOD have a GOD (creator) as Mary as a human did?

(5) And then later in Revelation, 3 where as JESUS says, He is the first BORN of Creation and witness of GOD".

"If JESUS was eternal God, how was he the "first born" of all of creation?

Well these five enigmatic verses were ignored or explained away by the majority of Christians (followers of JESUS). By about 320 AD, the overwhelming majority of Christians (at least 85 percent) and their Pastors and Leaders believed JESUS WAS GOD, GOD INCARNATE vs the lesser Arius Movement who claimed JESUS was a created divine being. Then came Constantine, the emperor of Rome.

CHAPTER THREE:
TRINITY OR BURN

Constantine, after having a "strange" dream where as with the CROSS he conquered all of his enemies in battle, he awakens and declares the small and persecuted religious Cult in Rome, whose symbol was the cross, the official Religion of the Roman Empire. Thus in 325 AD Christianity was reborn as a major world religion and with it the Roman Concept of God as The "Trinity".

Constantine knew fully well the power of Unity and the danger and weakness of Division. This is why in 325 AD Constantine set up the Council of Nicia. By overwhelming majority vote, JESUS was declared to be both the SON OF GOD and GOD THE SON, one third of an Everlasting Godhead that became forever known as The "Trinity".

"GOD THE FATHER, GOD THE SON, GOD THE SPIRIT, THREE AS ONE".

The exact wording of the Nicene Creed stated that, "Jesus is true God from true God, begotten not made, one being with the Father. This creed was somewhat convoluted, stating on one hand that JESUS was true GOD and on the other saying he was "begotten" not made, suggesting an origin for JESUS while the Father (GOD) has no origin or beginning. (It is presumed that JESUS as true God has no origin as well).

Arius and his movement were branded as heretics and worse and they quickly went underground to avoid the coming persecution. Claiming JESUS was less than TRUE GOD and denying The Trinity was punishable by death as Constantine protected Unity in his new religion at all costs.

Christians were and are told to accept The Trinity and the Words of The Nicene Faith by Faith and not to question this "truth". For those who did question, they did so at their own peril. I always say that I'm glad I was born today at the Time of The End and not back in the days of The Stake.

Throughout the next 1000 years, long after Arius was gone, individuals and small groups who believed JESUS was the Son of God and not "true God" were branded as "Heretics" and often faced extreme persecution such as torture and being burned at the stake as heretics, "in league with the devil". After all, if a woman denied that JESUS WAS GOD, that was clear sign of witchcraft and satan worship, right? And a few rounds of sadistic torture would later bring out a confession of her accused guilt.

Then came the Protestant Reformation with Martin Luther proclaiming JESUS AS GOD (i.e. Trinity) followed by a new wave of brutal persecution against anyone who thought JESUS was less than true God. It is estimated that Luther and his madmen burned or hanged at least 100,000 persons as witches and heretics, all because they did not accept JESUS AS GOD.

An accused witch and GOD DENIER would be hanged, burned at the stake or tied to a chair and dunked under water for ten minutes. If they drowned or burned (died) = this was the divine sign of a witch as "God would deliver the innocent".

In fact, Luther and his Trinity, also set the stage for the Nazi Holocaust as Luther hated Jews and called them "Spawns of Satan" as Jewish people denied JESUS as GOD and Messiah, a double "blasphemy" in Luther's Book of Madness. The Roman Catholic Church, not to be bested, accused all Jews as "Christ Killers", a label that also fueled the Holocaust and was not rescinded until 1968 at Vatican II.

In more recent years, any group or sect that did not believe JESUS WAS GOD was labeled a "Cult". The cult-list included two new sects, Jehovah Witness and The Mormons who believed that JESUS had an origin, that he was a perfect man, a man who lived a sinless life. Yet all, both the Churches who proclaim JESUS as GOD vs the "perfect" man sects, are all very much mistaken.

Well, since 325 AD, fear of persecution and being burned at the stake, kept most people from questing THE TRINITY, at least outwardly and publicly.

Now its time to make theological history and see once and for all, who JESUS truly is and what the phrase "SON OF GOD" truly means.

CHAPTER FOUR: PROBLEMS WITH THE TRINITY

Before we look at the Theological problems with God as the Christian "Trinity", I want to start with a very deep conversation I had a long time ago.

DIVINE CONVERSATION

I remember a long time ago, a six year old child (my next door neighbor) overheard me talking to someone about God and the Book of Revelation. Later, this child asked me a question.

"Harry, did God make all things?"

I replied, "Yes, God made the sky and the trees, everything."

Next, the child asked me, "Did God make us?"

I replied, "Yes God made us, he made you and me and your mommy and daddy, and everyone."

Then, this child became thoughtful and asked me a question, the most profound question that anyone can ever ask,

"Who Made God?"

This child asked this question because our logical mind, even at age six, knows that everything must have a beginning, a birth. If there is a clock, there must be a clockmaker, if there is a bird, it must come from an egg hatched from a female bird. So who made GOD?

The I gave this child the most profound answer I could ever give, "No one made God, he always was".

Well his astonished and shocked expression showed that he just understood The GLORY OF GOD, no one made GOD, He Always Was, He always existed, who then created all things.

This brings us to theology, old and new, and the definition of God and of origin.

DEFINING GOD:

Before I show you who JESUS truly is, we must define "God". In virtually all cultures and religions, "GOD" is defined as always existing, always being, always in existence and never a time when HE did not exist and he then created all things as the architect of the universe and all life i.e., GOD HAS NO ORIGIN, NO BIRTH, NO BEGINNING.

THE GLORY OF GOD.

The above definition of ORIGINLESS GOD was solidified in the western, Judeo-Christian Culture as GOD is defined as a Divine Being with a male gender, THE FATHER as opposed to a "she" or an "it" as the "creative force in all things = BUDDHISM = STAR WARS. Enter, The Christian Trinity".

Note the word "trinity" is not found in The Bible, not in the New or Old Testament. But the concept of The "Godhead" is (A FATHER – A SON – HOLY SPIRIT) which later became known as The Trinity or Triune God.

PROBLEMS WITH THE TRINITY

TRINITY = JESUS AS ETERNAL GOD, ALONGSIDE THE FATHER AND THE HOLY SPIRIT AS ETERNAL GOD.

JESUS AS GOD is problematic. If JESUS always existed as GOD, then we would have eternal THREE GODS: GOD THE FATHER- GOD THE SON and GOD THE HOLY SPIRIT.

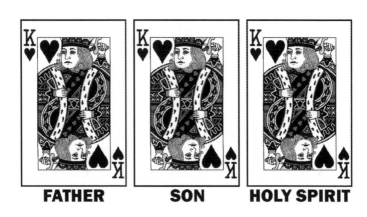

FATHER   SON   HOLY SPIRIT

These three playing Cards represent the Christian "Trinity"… always existing from eternity backwards.

Based upon our definition of GOD as WITHOUT ORIGIN, "always existing, always being, always in existence, JESUS AS GOD makes no sense. Any way you slice it, this represents Three ORIGIN-LESS (Eternal) Gods from everlasting backwards, GOD #1, GOD #2, GOD #3 renamed as GOD THE FATHER, GOD THE SON, GOD THE HOLY SPIRIT.

This Three ORIGIN-LESS GODS (IN ONE) concept seems to violate what GOD told us in Exodus, "HEAR

OH ISRAEL THE LORD YOUR GOD IS ONE GOD",
ONE ORGIN-LESS BEING.

This concept of The Trinity also contradicts much that
JESUS taught about God and THE FATHER and HIS
FATHER.

ARIUS AND HIS VERSES = REVISITED.

We also have the mysterious verses, highlighted by Arius
(and his movement) and quickly ignored, where as JESUS
refers to GOD as "MY GOD" and where JESUS said,
"The Father is greater than I".

YET as we have seen, by about 320, The Christian world
and their Churches accepted the Trinity, of GOD THE
FATHER, GOD THE SON, GOD THE SPIRIT, ALL
ETERNAL GOD AS ONE.

Now is time to break free of The Trinity and all of the
false views and analogies about GOD and see who JESUS
truly is.

CHAPTER FIVE:
THE CLONE OF GOD

I n Matt 15, Jesus asked his disciples "Who am I?

"Some said, "You are Elijah or Jeremiah. Then Peter proclaimed, 'You are the Christ, the Son of the living God.

JESUS then said to Peter, " Blessed are you Simon because you were revealed this from the father himself.

Note that GOD (The Father) believed that JESUS was his Son, not one third of an everlasting trinity.

So the question is, what does this phrase, "You are the Christ, the Son of the living God mean?

The ultimate clue rests in the most famous verse in the Gospel, John:3:16.

"For God so loved the world,
He gave his only begotten Son,
That whoever believes in Him
Will not perish but have
Everlasting life".

Again, JESUS states that He is the Son of God and the only-begotten, Son of God. In the Greek, which The Gospel was written, "only-begotten" means "mono-geneous", one time only, unique "birth".

THE CLONE OF GOD

To update "only begotten" and "mono-geneous" for 2010, we can say, JESUS IS THE ONE AND ONLY, CLONE OF GOD.

GOD the Father cloned JESUS, his son from himself. JESUS was not born with a mother or father, but He came forth from the father as a CLONE (mono-geneous) of His Father.

JESUS was not a clone as an earthly clone that needs genes from both a father and mother to exist from. You can only clone a goat if a goat first existed that came from male and female genetics.

JESUS was "cloned" from GOD THE FATHER and from the father alone, from His own divine molecular structure.

"For God so loved the world,
that he gave his only begotten
Son (cloned from himself) that
Whoever believes in (trusts in)
Will not perish but have
Everlasting life".

Isn't this exactly what JESUS said throughout The Gospel.

"The Father is greater than I".

"I can only do what The Father has shown me".

"That He came forth from The Father".

"That he was sent by The Father".

"That he only does the will of this Father".

In Rev:3:16, JESUS states that, "He is the first born of all Creation".

JESUS knew and proclaimed that He had an ORIGIN, A Birth. Jesus is saying that did not always exist and if it were not for the Father, JESUS would not exist = the first born of all creation.

This is exactly what JESUS as a CLONE of the Father would state, that he did not always exist and he had a "birth" or beginning or origin as the "Only Begotten" SON of God.

JESUS is the SON OF GOD in every sense of the word "son" as a Son proceeds from his Father and comes into existence because of his father.

Again, this is why JESUS states that "The Father is greater than I" because he knows were it not for the Father, he (Jesus) would not exist. Yet the Churches reject what JESUS said and proclaim GOD THE SON, one-third of an eternal (origin-less) trinity.

JESUS, as the divine CLONE OF GOD, always maintained he came from His Father and all that he learned was taught to him by his Father. He also said he was SENT BY HIS FATHER,

(GOD) To do the will of His Father and never his own will.

Summary

To be clear, here is exactly what I am saying which is exactly what JESUS was saying almost 2000 years ago,

"At one point in time, in pre-creation, all that existed was GOD The FATHER.

THE FATHER

Then God "cloned" his Son from Himself, as His *only begotten Son*, and then together they created the "heavens and the earth".

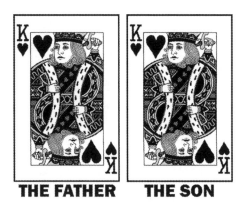

THE FATHER   **THE SON**

THE FATHER = GOD WITH NO BEGINNING = NO ORIGIN

JESUS = THE SON OF GOD = GOD WITH A BEGINNING, AN ORIGIN.

Again, here are my three simple, Playing Card Illustrations to better explain THE GODHEAD and what I am saying, well what JESUS has been saying all along.

FALSE TRINITY

FATHER   **SON**   **HOLY SPIRIT**

As we have seen, anyway you "slice" the Christian

"Trinity" it is three origin-less Gods from Everlasting, GOD #1, GOD #2, GOD #3.

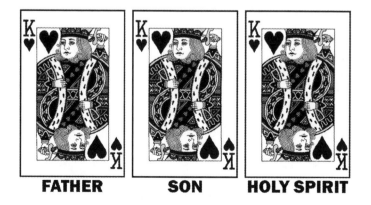

FATHER   **SON**   **HOLY SPIRIT**

This concept of "Trinity" that contradicts all that both The Old Testament and all that JESUS taught about God, His Father and is totally false.

PRE CREATION: ONE GOD

At one point in Pre-Creation, there was only GOD the FATHER, the one true origin-less, spiritual being from everlasting, from eternity backwards, The "I AM THAT I AM".

THE FATHER

GOD THE FATHER was all alone for HE alone existed. Then God decided to do the most amazing thing He ever did, even more amazing then His Creation of The Universe itself.

THE ONLY-BEGOTTEN SON = CLONE

Then at one "instant" in pre-creation, GOD "begat" A Son, a Clone of and from Himself and from that point forward, the SON = JESUS is Divine, GOD *with an origin*, the "I AM".

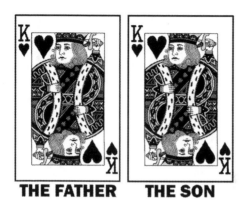

THE FATHER   THE SON

Then God declared,

"This is My Son, today
I have begotten you".
(ps:2:7).

The Holy Spirit was with GOD and His Son, again at a point in pre-creation, representing the true Biblical "Godhead". . . not the three "gods in one", all origin-less (false) "trinity".

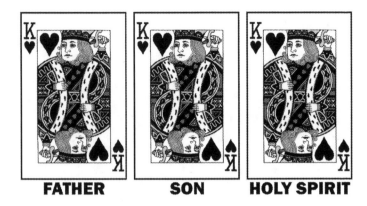

FATHER   **SON**   **HOLY SPIRIT**

We simply had to update and readjust our definition of GOD and His "Only Begotten" Son, in light of our knowledge of Cloning and of origin.

Now the question is this, Who exactly is JESUS?

What is the Clone of GOD?

CHAPTER SIX:
ORIGIN IS THE KEY

$$\equiv\!\!\!\equiv$$

So it seems that ARIUS was more right than not. True, JESUS had a birth, a beginning, an origin. Jesus was brought-into-existence as Arius claimed and the Nicene Creed states without a true explanation, "We believe in JESUS, the Son of God, True God, from true God, begotten not made".

Yet JESUS was the exact CLONE of His Father becoming *"GOD with An Origin"* (a unique concept that Arius and his followers didn't understand).

ONLY BEGOTTEN SON = *GOD WITH AN ORIGIN*

For almost 2000 years, we were forced to make a false choice, either JESUS was GOD THE SON, GOD (with no origin or beginning) or he was a perfected Man (with an origin, a beginning a birth).

The Truth is that JESUS as the SON OF GOD = *is GOD with an origin*, God with a beginning, a birth. This "impossibility" is possible as GOD cloned himself to "create" JESUS, HIS ONLY BEGOTTEN SON. (John:3:16) and THIS MAKES JESUS THE MOST UNIQUE BEING IN THE ENTIRE UNIVERSE!

DIVINITY- CLONED

A clone is a carbon- copy, an exact duplicate of what it came from. Its really quite simple, The Son or Clone of a dog is a dog, the son or clone of a lion is a lion and the Son or Clone of GOD = is GOD, *with an origin that is.*

GOD THE FATHER is God with no beginning, without origin. God always existed, always was, always is, the "I AM THAT I AM"= ever present.

JESUS, as the SON OF GOD = is *GOD with an origin*, with a birth, a beginning. "origin" is the difference between the father and the son, between JESUS and His Father.

If The Father did not exist, then the Son did not exist.

GOD THE FATHER IS ETERNAL GOD WITHOUT ORIGIN, WITHOUT A BEGINNING, HE ALWAYS WAS, THE EVER PRESENT ONE= "I AM THAT I AM".

JESUS AS THE "ONLY BEGOTTEN SON" OF GOD = GOD WITH AN ORIGIN, A BEGINNING. The instant that The Father "begat" His Son, JESUS became "I AM", divine and ever present.

Yet notice that JESUS called himself, "I AM" and not "I AM THAT I AM". . . the origin-less Title reserved for His Father and for Him Alone.

GOD THE FATHER = "I AM THAT I AM"

JESUS, HIS SON = "I AM".

JESUS was born, *the only begotten*, "cloned", *brought into existence* before creation and then He co-created all things with His Father.

So JESUS = is *God with an origin*, a true clone. This is why JESUS said, "if you have seen me you have seen the father" and "I and the father are one".

Again, this is why an instant after GOD "begot" (cloned) His Son, the instant after GOD brought His

Son into Existence, JESUS could declare, "I AM", EVER PRESENT, DIVINE, *GOD, WITH AN ORIGIN.*

This is why in Psalm 2, YHWH GOD declares the actual "birth", THE ORIGIN, the Cloning (begetting) of His Son, from Himself,

"You art my Son, Today
I have begotten you"

"Ask of Me and I will
Give you the nations
As your inheritance,
And the ends of the
Earth as your possession."
Ps:2:7.

"YHWH GOD also declares His Son, His only begotten CLONE is Divine, GOD (with an origin) in The Old Testament and echoed in the N.T. Book of Hebrews,

"Your throne, Oh God is
forever and ever," a
scepter of righteousness
is the scepter of your
kingdom",

and

"You have loved righteousness
and hated Lawlessness,
Therefore GOD, Your God,
Has anointed you."
PS: 45:6 & 7.

and

"Let all of the Angels
of God worship Him".
Deut:32:43.

GOD THE FATHER is declaring His Son, *whom he begot*, both GOD (divine) and HIS SON = "GOD, YOUR GOD, has annointed you". God also allows the angels to worship His Son proving His Son (JESUS) is Divine = GOD *with an origin.*

David, King of Israel, had a glimpse into this Mystery of JESUS' BIRTH when wrote from his vision,

"AND THE LORD SAID
UNTO MY LORD",

"Sit at my right hand
until I make your enemies
your footstool".
PS:110:1

Through out The Gospels, JESUS told Israel and the world that He had an origin, a beginning, a birthday but no one listened. Remember the mysterious verses that people just explained away or ignored to declare "Trinity"? Now these New Testament verses are crystal clear and make sense.

JESUS as the Divine CLONE & SON OF GOD would say the following as He knows He was brought into existence, origin, by GOD, HIS FATHER,

"There is none good but God who is one".

"The Father is greater than I".

"I come forth from The Father".

"I am the first born of creation
and the true witness of God".

"I am Alpha and Omega, the
First and the Last, the
Beginning and the End".

Now all of the mystical verses where JESUS said he had a GOD (= AN ORIGIN) makes complete sense, because the Father is truly His God as the Son did not always exist, he was "begotten", brought-into-existence by GOD HIMSELF as His Divine Son & Clone.

This is why JESUS said to Mary Magdalene and again in Revelation, that GOD was "MY GOD".

"I must ascend to your God and My God".

"My God, My God, why has thou forsaken Me".

"I am the first born of the creation of God"

"I will write the name of "My God"
upon your forehead".

JESUS has a beginning, *AN ORIGIN* as He is The CLONE of GOD in every sense of the word "Clone" = exact duplicate, of THE FATHER. He is also the truest Clone & SON as No mother was needed, JESUS came from the Father-Himself. Again, this is exactly what JESUS said.

"I came forth from The Father".

JESUS as the Divine Clone is the mirror image of His Father with one exception, JESUS has a birthday, an origin, while God The Father is origin-less, He always existed and is the TRUE FATHER of JESUS and . . . JESUS is the true SON OF GOD in every aspect of the word "son".

This is what we read in The Gospel of John,

"In the beginning, was The Word
and the Word was with God and
the Word was God = divine."

In the beginning, before creation, JESUS was with His Father and Jesus is Divine. More specifically,

GOD THE FATHER = is GOD with no origin or beginning

JESUS, The SON OF GOD = God with *AN ORIGIN*, a birth, a beginning, Cloned from The Father Himself, before Creation.

GOD doesn't need a mirror, all he Has to do is look at his Son and HE Sees himself.

Now, every verse about JESUS AS MESSIAH (Christ) and His Father in The Old Testament Bible makes complete and total sense. As the SON OF GOD = THE CLONE OF GOD as

JESUS IS EMANNUEL = "GOD WITH US"

"Behold, a virgin shall bear a
child and shall call his name
Emmanuel" which means "God with us".
(Isa:7:14).

When JESUS returns at the End of the coming Great Tribulation of seven years, He shall be called "EMMANUEL" "God with Us" and JESUS as the Divine Clone and Son of God will be exactly that, GOD WITH US (God with an origin that is).

"And He "Messiah" shall be called
Wonderful, Counselor, mighty god,
Everlasting Father, prince of
Peace". Isa:9:6

JESUS, as Messiah, as the true Son and Clone of GOD would fulfill Isa:9 as He is the mirror image of His father. Notice JESUS is called the "prince of peace" because He came from and after His Father, The King. (another hidden reference to the mystical but real origin of JESUS, Messiah).

Psalm 2: says (revisited) where as GOD THE FATHER declares, "You art my Son, today I have begotten you" and then adds,

"Kiss the son and trust in Him
lest a curse come upon you.

The Old Testament also tells us to "trust in God alone".

Therefore, JESUS as the true Son and Clone of GOD can be trusted as He is divine, the mirror image of His father, GOD *with an origin.*

JOHN:3:16 revisited

JESUS as the true son and clone of GOD, then being made man and dying for the sins of the world takes on a new depth and meaning as JESUS is truly God's Son in every aspect of the word SON. This great Sacrifice of The Father (Jn:3:16) takes on a deeper meaning as God truly gave his own Son to be killed for the sins of the world. The Prayer of JESUS after the last supper takes on a whole new meaning as well when we realize JESUS is the true Son and clone of GOD.

JESUS fell on his face and prayed in the Garden of Gethsemane, "Father, if there is any way this cup may pass, but not my will but thy will be done".

JESUS prayed as a true Son to His Father and accepted his fate, to be led as a Lamb to the slaughter. A brutal beating and torture death, very well portrayed in the movie THE PASSION. Jesus as one-third of the false, origin-less Trinity is not really much of a sacrifice of GOD at all.

Finally, this is why JESUS said (to Israel) in Zechariah: 12, that,"I, The Lord shall save you and they shall look upon ME who they pierced". It was JESUS THE SON OF GOD who died for the sins of the world on the cross (i.e. pierced) and not God The Father, who made JESUS = LORD – ADONAI= GOD *with an origin*, a true SON in every sense of the word.

The HOLY SPIRIT

It is not clear exactly when the Holy Spirit came into existence? As He is the Spirit of the Father and The Son, this may mean that the Holy Spirit was "born" the instant that JESUS was cloned, brought into existence, as the Only begotten Son of God. Proverbs six seems to state that the Holy Spirit (as the Spirit of wisdom) "existed with God in the beginning before creation". I believe JESUS was "born" and then the Holy Spirit followed as the Spirit of the Father and The Son.

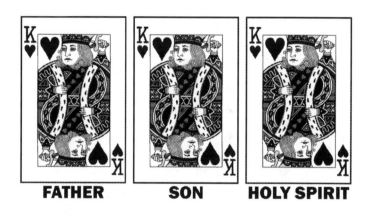

FATHER   SON   HOLY SPIRIT

And if God "cloned" The Holy Spirit from Himself and then later CLONED = BEGAT A SON from Himself next, that is all right too and this brings us to another Mystery, The NAME OF GOD.

CHAPTER SEVEN:
THE NAME OF GOD

"What is God's Name? and
What is His Son's Name?
Does anyone know?
Prov:30:4

Even in the Book of Proverbs, we are told that God
has a SON and now we know exactly what this
3000 year old text means, that GOD has a true Son, a
true CLONE, (God with an origin) His Only-Begotten
Son, JESUS (Jn:3:16). Now as we have made history in
solving this Mystery, lets make history once more and
solve the Mystery as to the mystical name of God.

Contrary to popular belief, I do not believe that the
mystical name of GOD is "YAHWEH" or "JEHOVAH"
or "YESHUAH"

BACK STORY: For approx 1500 years, from Moses to Jesus, the true name of GOD was hidden and unspoken through out Ancient Israel. Then JESUS began his ministry and everything radically changed. Remember in ancient Israel and in Jesus' day, the Hebrews spoke Hebrew and Aramaic, a slang form of Hebrew and most people could not read or write Hebrew. This was the role of the scribes, rabbis and Pharisees.

CIRCA 0 AD, as Isa:7:14, predicted, The Angel came to Mary (speaking in Hebrew) and told Mary of the Virgin Birth and to name her miracle son, "YE-SHU-AH" (JESUS in English) which means "GOD SAVES" or "SALVATION". Encoded within the name "YESUAH" is hidden 3 of the 4 mystical Letters for God's name = YHVH or YOD-HEI-VAV-HEI (in Hebrew).

For 30 years, JESUS was known as "YESHUAH" the Carpenter from Nazareth, until he started his ministry after being Baptized at the River Jordan by John The Baptist. Then JESUS changed the pronunciation of his name from "YE-SHU-AH" to "YA-SHU-AH" and announced, "I COME IN MY FATHER'S NAME". (Jn:5:43). This is the major clue in learning God's true name as all 4 letters of the YHWH are encoded within the name "YAH-SHU-AH" which I will now prove is the true and hidden, NAME FOR GOD (I posted this information, the true name of God, on our site on APRIL 01 2010).

THE ADVENTURE BEGINS

It is believed (and written) that GOD HIMSELF wrote and gave The Torah to Moses This means that GOD hid HIS HOLY NAME until the time it was to be revealed BY HIS OWN SON. (I also believe this to be true as it explains The Bible Code. Moses did not have computers or advanced knowledge of computer ELS skip codes.

In the ancient Hebrew Text of The Torah (five Books of Moses) the name of GOD is written (hidden) without certain key letters so this name could not be pronounced and spoken. In Hebrew, the name of GOD is written as YOD - HEI - VAV - HEI (as Hebrew is read "backwards", from right to left).

This mystical name (for GOD)is known as the "Tetragrammaton" (YOD-HEI-VAV-HEI) and is correctly translated into English = YHVH.

When we read our English translated Bibles, we read The LORD GOD and "LORD" is a substitute for YHVH = YOD - HEI - VAV - HEI, the hidden Hebrew name of GOD.

YHVH is known that the abbreviated name for GOD in ancient Hebrew was "YAH" (as revealed in Ps:68). The name ELIYAH (ELIJAH) means "YAH IS GOD".

Back in medieval times, some leading English Scholars (of Hebrew) mistakenly translated YHVH (YOD- HEI-VAV- HEI) to YHWH substituting a "w" for a "v" as a probable translation.

These scholars then took YHWH and added the vowels "a" and "e" and came up with YAH-WEH which they pronounced as "YAH-WAY" which has a nice flowing sound in English and who really knows ancient Hebrew anyway.

I BELIEVE THAT "YAHWEH" CANNOT
BE THE ANCIENT HEBREW NAME FOR
GOD AND HERE IS WHY.

1) The Hidden Name of GOD is YHVH and not YHWH. There is no "w" in = the hidden, Hebrew name for God. VAV is a "v" sound and not "w".

The Letter "W" does not exist in the Hebrew Alphabet that only contains 22 letters. In Ancient Hebrew, there is no sound pronounced as "WAY". So there is NO WAY that the Name of GOD could be "YAH-WAY".

In ancient Hebrew, there is one, limited sound for

"W". It is written as a double "VAV" = VAV-VAV and is pronounced as "WAW" as in WAWA. Applied to the YHVH, that would be pronounced "YA-WA" not YAHWEH or YAH-WAY. Some scholars even argue that an extra VAV is the missing Letter in The Tetragrammton

YHVH GOD as "YAWA" cannot be true for two reasons. 1) In Hebrew, WAW" (VAV-VAV) cannot be followed by a HEI (H sound) as is found in YOD-HEI-VAV-HEI. (just as in English, a "b" cannot be followed by a "w").

YA-WA or (YAHWEH) cannot be the ancient name

for GOD because ALL Hebrew names have a meaning and YA-WA or (YAHWEH) has no meaning.

NOAH = RESPITE,
ADAM = MAN & RUDDY,
EVE = MOTHER OF ALL

THE CORRECT ENGLISH TRANSLATION of YOD-HEI-VAV-HEI = Y H V H and there is no "W" in the YHVH in any way, shape or form.

YEHOVAH or JEHOVAH

Around 1100 AD, Masoretic Jewish Scholars took the English spelling of ADONAI = LORD in Hebrew and applied these vowels: A - O - A to YHVH, the Mystery name of GOD and got: Y a H o V a H.

Y A H O V A H was later Anglicized to JEHOVAH yet there is not a "J" letter or sound in Hebrew.

This was a really cool theological concept, but is "YAHOVAH" the True name of GOD? Not according to JESUS it isn't, (close but "no cigars" as they say).

NAME OF GOD: PART 2

JESUS said this in the Gospel of John

"I COME IN MY FATHER'S NAME
AND YOU DO NOT RECEIVE ME.
ONE SHALL COME IN HIS OWN
NAME (Antichrist) AND HIM
YOU SHALL RECEIVE."
(JN:5:43)

(Translated into English) JESUS is actually telling us that his name is not JESUS but that JESUS is His Father's Name. Now let's look at the Name of God = JESUS in

Hebrew for in this ancient language is where the mystery of YHVH is formulated and solved.

JESUS is the Greek to Latin to English Translation of his Hebrew name. The Hebrew name that JESUS actually came in is "YESHUAH" commonly pronounced "YI-SHU-AH" which means "SALVATION" or "God Saves". Here is what "YE-SHU-AH" (Jesus) looks like in Hebrew, in its long form, the shorter form lacks the last letter- HEI

Notice this name "YESHUAH" contains three of the four letters of the "YHVH" of the name of GOD (Tetragrammaton). ALL THAT IS MISSING IS THE FIRST "HEI" (H).

Watch what happens when we add the missing "HEI" from the "YHVH" to YESHUAH, the Hebrew name for JESUS.

Now its time for some Theological "magic".

ARE YOU READY? ABRA-KADABRA...

3

2

1

PRESTO!!! The Tetragrammton, The mystical name of GOD (YHVH) is encoded right in the Hebrew name of JESUS all along, within the name, "YESHUAH". . .

Another way to view this is to add the Hebrew letters, SHIN (s) and AYIN (A) to the mystical YHVH to form "YA-SHU-AH" and something far, far more.

FAR DEEPER MEANING

There is much more to this story as when we add the HEI to YESHUAH this changes both the pronunciation and meaning of the word. Now it becomes "YAH-SHU-AH", taking the shortened Hebrew name for GOD = YAH and adding SHU-AH = the word that forms salvation

The hidden name of God (YAH-SHU-AH) becomes personalized as "GOD (HIMSELF) IS OUR SALVATION" and not just a generalized, SALVATION or GOD SAVES = YESHUAH.

This is what JESUS was teaching us in The Lord's Prayer, "OUR FATHER WHO ART IN HEAVEN, HALLOWED BE THY NAME".

OUR FATHER = YAH-SHU-AH = GOD IS OUR SALVATION

Summary: so with the YHVH (Tetragrammton) there were two letters missing, SHIN (s) and AYIN (a) to form the name of GOD = "YAH-SHU-AH" and in the Hebrew name YE-SHU-AH (JESUS) there was one letter missing, a HEI (H) to form the hidden Name of God = "YAH-SHU-AH".

YAH-SHU-AH GOD, THE FATHER, hid HIS true name in "YHVH" (YHWH) in a mystery, to be revealed by His very own SON, YESHUAH, THE MESSIAH.

YAH-SHU-AH was right under the noses of the Scholars and Theologians and they failed to see this. Instead they made the mistake of writing God's name as YHWH, then YAHWEH and pronouncing it as "YAHWAY" or mistakenly claiming God's Name is YAHOVAH or JEHOVAH.

GOD HAS A TRUE HEBREW NAME AS
THIS IS THE LANGUAGE HE GAVE UNTO MEN.

So the true name of GOD (THE FATHER) in HEBREW
IS "YAH-SHU-AH" (YHVH) and cannot really be
translated into English (nor should it be) and the closest
English Translation is YESHUAH = JESUS.

important note: You may still believe that it is somewhat
trivial in that adding one letter (HEI) is that relevant,
that pronouncing the Hebrew name of Jesus as "YAH-
SHU-AH" vs "YE-SHU-AH" has that much importance.
Well beyond the translation of the name changing from
GOD SAVES (YESHUAH) to GOD IS MY (OUR)
SALVATION (YAHSHUAH) take a look at this.

It is the difference between calling your human father,
HARRY, "A Father of a child or children" vs HARRY,
HE IS MY FATHER.

Or look at "YA-SHU-AH" vs YE-SHU-AH" in this way.

Say you have a little five year old boy and every time
he tastes or sees a food that he doesn't like he yells out,

"YUCK", "YUCK". When in school at lunchtime, the teachers think its kind of amusing to see Johnny yelling out "YUCK, "YUCK" when he sees a food he dislikes. But what happens when we change one letter, when we change the "Y" to an "F"...?... see my point?

OR LOOK AT IT THIS WAY. NAME A CHILD "DOLPH" AND HE HAS AN INTERESTING NAME, ADD AN "A" = ADOLF AND THE CHILD IS STIGMATIZED AND DEMONIZED FOR LIFE.

So it is clear to see how just one letter changed or added can radically change the meaning of a word or phrase and this is the same with The Name of God.

I am positive that JESUS changed and pronounced his name "YAH-SHU-AH" vs "YE-SHU-AH". I am also sure his disciples called him "YAH-SHU-AH" as well. Again, this may seem trivial to us today but to the Pharisees, the Hebrew Scribes and Scholars of JESUS' day, this difference in pronunciation had a dramatic difference that sealed his fate and doom and here is why.

NOW FOR THE FIRST TIME IN ALMOST 1500 YEARS, THE TRUE NAME OF GOD WAS SPOKEN IN ANCIENT ISRAEL, NOT ONLY USED BY JESUS BUT BY HIS DISCIPLES AND THE MASSES AS WELL, THE BLIND, CRIPPLES, PROSTITUTES AND ALL MANNER OF "SINNERS", SPEAKING THE HOLY NAME OF GOD AND CALLING YESHUAH (JESUS) BY THAT SACRED NAME AS WELL!!

The Pharisees knew that "YAH-SHU-AH" was the mystical name of GOD- REVEALED = YHVH and that JESUS was claiming to be THE SON OF GOD = "YAH-SHU-AH" = AND COMING IN HIS FATHER'S NAME which The Pharisees saw as Blasphemy and Sacrilege.

JESUS was revealing the hidden, mystical and sacred name of GOD to all, to the lowly uneducated masses, to the common folk, in both pronunciation "YAH-SHU-AH" and in his statement (below) and this enraged the Pharisees. In their pride and thinking, only they were privileged to this hidden, rabbinical knowledge.

"I COME IN MY FATHER'S NAME
AND YOU DO NOT RECEIVE ME.
ONE SHALL COME IN HIS OWN
NAME (Antichrist) AND HIM
YOU SHALL RECEIVE."
(JN:5:43)

Jesus speaking the name "YAH-SHU-AH" is lost in our modern day translation, theology and reading of the English Text of the Gospel, but it was not lost to the Pharisees and Scribes and filled them with rage!

Again, this is why the Pharisees accused JESUS of "Blasphemy", by claming to be THE SON OF GOD and EQUAL TO GOD as HE COMES IN HIS FATHER'S NAME = "YAH-SHU-AH".

SO THE MYSTICAL AND TRUE NAME
OF GOD IS "YAH-SHU-AH" AND
NOT YAHWEH or JEHOVAH

AND IT WAS FOUND IN THE GOSPEL
OF JOHN:5:43 ALL ALONG!

FINAL QUESTION: WHAT IS JESUS' NAME?

If JESUS CAME IN HIS FATHER'S NAME
WHAT IS HIS NAME? WHAT IS THE NAME
OF THE SON OF GOD, THE MESSIAH?

"Behold. A Virgin shall conceive
and bear a son and shall call
His Name, EMMANUEL which
translates to "God With Us".
(Is:7:14).

JESUS NAME = EMMANUEL = GOD WITH US =
THE TRUE SON & CLONE OF GOD- HIMSELF.

There is some confusion to the above verse (Isa:7:14) as Mary did not name her son "Emmanuel" but "YE-SHU-AH" (JESUS). In the Hebrew text, it implies that "He" = GOD will name his Son "Emmanuel" and not the virgin, Mary.

"Behold. A Virgin shall conceive
and bear a son and (HE)shall call
His Name, EMMANUEL which
translates to "God With Us".
(Is:7:14).

If Mary would have named the baby JESUS (Yeshuah) by the name, "EMMANUEL", her and Joseph would have probably been stoned to death for Blasphemy. (The name "YESHUAH" was used by Hebrew People and is "JOSHUAH" when translated into English and again means "GOD SAVES".

The "Emmanuel" Equivalent today would be if a Moslem Family in Saudi Arabia named their baby boy, "ALLAH". They would be stoned to death for Blasphemy.

Another modern example is if a family deep down in the Bible Belt of Alabama, USA, named their baby boy, SATAN. Youth Social Services would accuse the parents of child abuse and satanic ritual, the infant would be removed from the home and this would be a major story on FOX news.

ANCIENT SUMMARY

(6-0 B.C.E.) GOD in His Wisdom, told Mary to name her baby "YE-SHU-AH" (JESUS) so that when he grew up and started His Messianic Ministry (at age 30) He would pronounce His name as "YAH-SHU-AH" and announce that He comes in His Father's name" and reveal this sacred name OF GOD unto all.

ANCIENT UPDATE

(2017 AD -2020 AD) When "YAH-SHU-AH" MESSIAS (GOD'S MESSIAH) returns to earth at The End of The Great Tribulation (seven years) to destroy the Antichrist and save the remnant of Israel, His Name shall be called EMMANUEL, "GOD WITH US." (Zech:8:13 = Rev:19).

DURING THE MILLENNIUM, JESUS WILL BE KNOWN AS EMMANUEL = "GOD WITH US", GOD *WITH AN ORIGIN* that is.

JESUS Himself tells us this in Revelation;

"And I shall write upon Him
the name of My Father (YAHSHUAH)
and the Name of the City of
MY GOD which is New Jerusalem
And My New Name, a name that I
am not known by."
(Rev:3:12)

(* notice that Jesus says, "and the name of the city of "MY GOD". Jesus again is saying that HE has a GOD, a "begetter" a person who brought him into existence, GOD HIS FATHER).

Although JESUS is acknowledged as "EMMANUEL", this is not the name that He has been known by and called by for the last 1950 + years.

So, in light of this Revelation of God's Name, who do we pray to and what name do we use?

It is very simple as our prayer does not really change, it is our knowledge of Scripture and our understanding of God's name that changes and has been enhanced and perfected.

We pray as JESUS taught us in The Lord's Prayer, OUR FATHER, WHO ART IN HEAVEN, HALLOWED BE THY NAME. Now we just know exactly what his NAME IS = "YAH-SHU-AH" = "GOD IS OUR SALVATION" and DO NOT TAKE HIS NAME IN VAIN as this is The Third of The Ten Commandments.

We must know his name in order to
Not take His Name in vain.

And when we pray for help and healing, we end our prayer in JESUS NAME (ENGLISH) but I believe in Light of this "Revelation", we should end our prayer in The true, Hebrew Name of GOD, "YAH-SHU-AH".

Now it seems that GOD was not the only "person" who cloned a Son from Himself... for it seems Satan, the devil, wanted to copy what God did as well.

CHAPTER EIGHT:
APOCALYPSE 2012

⸻

If you are familiar with Satan, the devil, he is the ultimate copycat and GOD wanna-be. Satan as Lucifer was cast from Heaven because he wanted to be God and sit upon the throne of God (ISA:14). Satan led a war against God and was cast from heaven to earth, along with one-third of the angels, now demons, who joined in Lucifer's rebellion.

CLONE WARS

Satan knows that JESUS is the SON of GOD and the CLONE OF GOD and in the ultimate act of imitating God, I believe that The Antichrist, The Beast of Rev:13 will be a Clone as well. Back in 1980, Scientists discovered the lost tomb of Osiris, an Egyptian god who was said to have died and was or will be Resurrected. Archeologists found this underground coffin of Osiris in an empty pool. The walls were surrounding the pool were three feet high and at one time held an unknown liquid that was gone.

The Coffin of Osiris was nine feet long and was reported to be empty, but what if it wasn't? It is my theory that this tomb contained a gigantic mummy, over seven ft tall with preserved of clonable DNA. Over the past 30 years, as part of a secret program, there could have been 10,000 Clones of this ancient Giant until one was perfect. A perfect physical being that hated God and loved Satan, The Antichrist. I believe God calls him "The Beast" in Rev:13 because as a Clone, he lacks a human conscience and is a psychopath with no feeling, empathy or compassion. He will speak of brotherhood and peace, but in his heart, he is a monster, a serial killer, THE BEAST.(Rev:13).

An alternate (clone) theory I have is that Satan preserved a Vial of Cain's Blood, hidden in the frozen mountains of Tibet. This could have been found via a secret map leading to Cain's Blood, the Blood of the First Murderer (cain killed his brother, Abel) who will be cloned as Antichrist, The Beast of Revelation:13.

You can read more of my Antichrist theory, who he is and what he comes as in my book, JUNE 6 2006, 666, Antichrist revealed or read it on our site @ http:/www.satansrapture.com and satansrapture.org. Contrary to popular myth, Antichrist does not come as a western politician or President in a three piece suit. Antichrist comes (in a white robe) as the savior of all religions, faiths and creeds. He will come

As the 5th Buddha, world teacher whose personal name is MAITREYA which calculates to 666 in the ancient Hebrew Alphabet. (See Rev:13:18).

It is also possible that the False Prophet is a CLONE as well, A clone of JESUS. We read that The False Prophet, "comes as a Lamb and speaks as a dragon". That would be a cloned JESUS as the LAMB OF GOD who speaks as a dragon, a demon or satan himself. For all we know, clonable DNA was removed from the Shroud of Turin, to clone JESUS as the False prophet to Israel.

CHAPTER NINE:
FINAL CHURCH – TRUE CHURCH

I do believe that we are living at the time of The End, and there is a 99.9999 chance that the Tribulation will start before DEC 21 2012, the day the ancient Mayan Calendar of 5000 years ends. This is based upon the fact that Israel must attack Iran to stop their nuclear program and Israel said they have until 2011 (completes) to stop Iran.

In the parable of the Fig Tree in Matt:24:52, JESUS taught of a final generation that will see the Apocalypse (tribulation). On 14 MAY 1948, Israel was miraculously re-born as a nation. (June 1967 Israel recaptured Jerusalem their ancient capital). When we add 70 years, a complete generation (vs a forty year generation) we get 2018.

1948 + 70 = 2018 minus seven years (Tribulation) = 2011. . . and 2011 is the year Israel said they have to stop Iran's nuclear threat or they will be vaporized.

Now with the Doomsday Clock ticking down, this brings us back to our revelation of who JESUS truly is, the only begotten SON and CLONE OF HIS FATHER, GOD.

FULL CIRCLE

We have seen in Matt:16, JESUS asked his Disciples who He is, and Peter replied, "YOU ARE THE CHRIST, THE SON OF THE LIVING GOD". Then Jesus agreed to Peter and said unto him, "Blessed are you peter, for the Father himself has revealed this truth unto you".

Peter was shown the great truth and mystery, that JESUS is truly the "Only-Begotten" SON and CLONE of His Father, becoming *God with an origin*, whom GOD His Father has anointed him both Lord and Christ (Messiah).

Next, JESUS goes on to say to Simon, "You Simon shall be called Peter and upon this rock I will build My Church".

Here Jesus said, "UPON THIS ROCK = THIS TRUTH OF WHO HE IS" = becomes the cornerstone of His Church, where as all who believe this truth, that "JESUS IS THE CHRIST, THE SON OF THE LIVING GOD" become a stone, a living, breathing stone in the true Church of God.

Note, it is not Peter who is the cornerstone (as the Roman Catholic Church would mistakenly believe) but the TRUTH and revelation of who JESUS is, that Peter was shown, that becomes the Rock and cornerstone of God's true Church upon earth. Then Jesus goes on to describe his true church, based upon the TRUTH that JESUS IS THE CHRIST, THE SON AND CLONE OF THE TRUE AND LIVING GOD",

"And I shall give you the keys
of the Kingdom, and what you
loose on earth shall be
loosened in heaven and
what you bind on earth
shall be loosened in
heaven,"

"And even the gates of hell
shall not prevail against
thee".

Wow! Is that a heavy statement or what? His Church, all who believe that JESUS IS THE CHRIST, THE SON AND CLONE OF THE LIVING GOD, will have the keys of The Kingdom, the very keys to unlock the POWER OF GOD.

The true Church will have the power to BIND sickness, disease, Satan and his demons and LOOSEN or RELEASE Forgiveness and Healing from heaven.

Further, JESUS said that his True Church will have power over the gates (powers) of Hell itself, power over Satan = and this is why we can bind and cast out satan and his fallen angels = demons.

THEN AND NOW

If we take one honest look at Christianity through-out the ages up until today, 2010, we see the complete opposite of what JESUS said. We see a Church, Catholic, starting in 325 AD , to Protestant (1500 AD) to today (2010) VOID of the power of God and power-less against Satan and his demons.

When was the last time that you went to a Church and saw the Power of God released in a miraculous way? When was the last time you saw true healing and miracles happening in any church, as we read of in the Gospels and The Book of Acts? WE DON'T and the reason is the Churches since 100 AD through 325 Ad (Catholic Churches) through The Protestant Reformation (1500) to today are based and built upon a falsehood, The origin-less and twisted TRINITY and not upon the Truth of Who JESUS is.

TRUTH OF GOD = POWER OF GOD

FALSEHOOD = NO POWER OF GOD

THE FINAL CHURCH

I believe that all who accept the truth of Who JESUS is,

"YOU ARE THE CHRIST AND SON (CLONE)
OF THE LIVING GOD",

become a rock, a living, breathing stone in this Spiritual Church and when we gather-together with two or three other true believers (in this truth) then we are part of The TRUE CHURCH that Jesus came to build and the POWER of GOD will be released in our "church" in a miraculous way. We will see healing and miracles today, just as believers saw in the Days when JESUS had his ministry and when the First Church was started in Jerusalem, in Acts.

JESUS predicted this final and true Church in Matt:18 and in the Book of Revelation.

"Where two or three are
gathered in My Name,
there I AM, in your
midst". (Mt:18:20)

"And what two or three
agree upon on earth
shall be done unto
them from heaven".

To "gather in His Name" = means to gather = or assemble in HIS TRUTH, the truth of who JESUS IS, "YOU ART THE CHRIST, THE SON OF THE LIVING GOD". the true SON and CLONE OF GOD, *GOD with an origin.*

Notice that JESUS breaks his Church = his assembly = his gathering = down to the lowest common denominator possible for a gathering, "two or three", YOU and ONE or TWO other true believers and followers of JESUS.

GOD knows that at this Time of the End, (NOW) the Churches will be riddled and filled with false doctrines and lies, starting with THE LIE of THE TRINITY that virtually every "Christian" Church is built and based upon. The Jehovah Witness and Mormons have built their Church upon the REVERSE-LIE (sinking sand) of JESUS as a "perfect" man, a concept that does not exist because if Jesus was just human = he is imperfect. This seems to be an exact repeat of the rebellion of Ancient Israel and God's Warnings thru Jeremiah, the Prophet,

"An astonishing and horrible thing
has occurred in the land, the

Prophets have prophesized falsely,
The Priests rule by their own power,
AND MY PEOPLE LOVE IT SO. But
What will be they do at their
Latter End (End Times?).
Jere:5:20.

If JESUS said where 20 or 10 or even 4 or 5 believers "gather in His Name" (TRUTH) he may never have an assembly or Church after 325 AD. But "two or three" makes it possible for us ALL to re-start and become a part of the True Church of God, *"His Faithful Remnant."*

REVELATION:3

To the Church of Philadelphia

[8]I know thy works: behold, I have set before thee an open door, and no man can shut it: for thou hast a little power, and hast kept my word, and hast not denied my name.

[10]Because thou hast kept the word of my patience, I also will keep thee from the hour of temptation, which shall come upon all the world, to try them that dwell upon the earth.

Again, the Church of Philadelphia was and is a small gathering = i.e. "you have a little power". But they have the TRUTH of GOD, starting with The TRUTH OF

WHO JESUS IS… and they will have the power of God in their midst.

The Church of Philadelphia is the only Church = group of believers = who will ESCAPE the coming Tribulation = in the First of TWO RAPTURES = when they are TAKEN = through their OPEN DOOR = INTO HEAVEN! Read the letters to the seven churches, only the Church of Philadelphia was given an OPEN DOOR (reward) for their faithfully Keeping God's Word in purity & practice and under hardship, tribulation patience (perseverance).

The other six churches (In Revelation chapters 2 & 3) were rebuked and told to repent of sins and patterns of sin or they will be LEFT BEHIND and "cast into Great Tribulation".

Now, as in the Days of Old with ancient Israel, every believer today has a choice to make, of what path they will choose to walk down in light of this "revelation" of who JESUS truly is, The Son and Clone of God The Father.

WARNING: turning this page will change your life forever. Failure to turn this page will have already changed your life in a negative and God-less way.

CHAPTER TEN:
TWO PATHS: CHOOSE LIFE
THE APOSTLES CREED

U PDATE: 21 AUG 2010, as I write this very page, Russia is loading fuel rods into Iran's first nuclear reactor that will go "hot", online in this dark and historic day and threat to the very survival of the Nation of Israel, to God's own people.

I believe that before DEC 21 2012 AD, the ancient Mayan "Doomsday" in their 5000 year calendar, the Great Tribulation (Apocalypse) will start. Between 2011 into 2012 (at the latest) Israel must and will attack Iran to end Iran's nuclear threat and when they do, this will trigger a great war, starting in the Mid-east against Israel which will explode into an Islamic Holy War against the West (USA, Canada & Europe) when Hamas detonates the Dome of the Rock Mosque (in Jerusalem) and blames Israel and the western nations who support her.

Waves of global terror Attacks will trigger the Crash of all world economies and total CHAOS. . . leading to the First of Two Raptures (for the true followers of JESUS) followed by the coming of Antichrist as the world teacher and savior of all religions, faiths and creeds.

The Doomsday Clock is truly ticking down to Apocalypse!

In the Shadow of the coming Apocalypse, we can become part of God's true Church, His Faithful Remnant, to become a part of God's Final Move before the Tribulation starts.

Remember, the First Church was started upon a wave of signs, wonders, miracles and healings and I believe the Final Church, God's Faithful Remnant, will be followed by the same signs, wonders and miracles and then "caught-up" (rapture) into Heaven as a Final WITNESS unto all.

APOSTLES CREED

TWO CHOICES::: CHOOSE LIFE:

With this End Times Revelation of who JESUS truly is, you have the opportunity to become Part of JESUS True Church, the Church of Philadelphia, *His Faithful Remnant*, to follow JESUS in Spirit and Truth and be "accounted worthy" to ESCAPE the coming tribulation in the First of Two Raptures.

Lu:21:34-36 = Mt:24:40-44 = Rev:3:10

By Accepting the truth of WHO JESUS IS, you have chosen LIFE, you have chosen to become a living stone in God's true Church, you have placed yourself on the Path to heaven, that straight and narrow path that leads to eternal life.

HOUSES BUILT UPON SAND

The falsehood and heresy that permeates the Churches doesn't end with the false 'Trinity" "or perfect man falsehood, it just begins. The majority of Protestant Churches today such as Baptist, Assemblies of God, many Pentecostal Churches, Lutheran, Evangelical also believe and embrace the LIE of OSAS = "Once Saved, Always Saved" or Salvation by faith Alone. (a virtual "license to sin", to basically do whatever you want and delude yourself that you are 'saved" guaranteed heaven and a rapture in the air".

The catholic churches (Roman, Orthodox, Anglican and Armenian) also have built their Houses on the "sinking sand" of the TRINITY LIE, and also pervert Salvation into Guaranteed Heaven through the falsehood of Infant baptism and trust in ritual. In conclusion, all Churches are based upon THE TRINITY LIE and then slide further into darkness, from OSAS to infant baptism and worse. An example is the false, "Faith Prosperity" doctrine of the Protestants, the "name it, claim it" delusion.

APOSTLES CREED

We read in Acts two that the early church met for prayer and breaking bread and in following the Apostle's Creed. We also read of the signs, wonders and miracles and healings that followed this early and first Church as they walked in The Truth. They may not have fully understood what the SON OF GOD meant? But they did not twist and corrupt The Truth into the Lie of The Roman Trinity, nor did they allow their Children to believe the Lie of Santa Claus, to later have their first faith shattered as glass and forever have this lie associated with JESUS, Christmas and Christianity.

Here is the Apostles Creed, updated for 2010, that represents the simple truth of Jesus' Gospel, The Creed of The True Church, that Jesus came to build.

(1) We believe that
"JESUS IS THE CHRIST
The Son of The Living God"
(Matt:16:16

(2) We believe in Repentance
and Baptism in JESUS Name for
The Forgiveness of Sin and
The Gift of The Holy Spirit.
(Acts 2:38.)

(3)We Are Called to a
"New Life in Christ",
In The Power of His Spirit,
To Follow His Teachings of
Love, Forgiveness and Mercy
(Matt:7:21/Jn:13:34-35)

(4)Jesus Promised To Bring Us
To Heaven, To His Father's
Kingdom, If We Continue to
Follow His Teachings, if
We keep His Word with
Perseverance.(Rev:3:10)
(Jn:10:27/Jn:14:2.)

END TIMES UPDATE:
The Believers who truly
Follow JESUS will be
"Accounted Worthy" To
Escape The Coming Tribulation
In The First of Two Raptures.
(Lu:21:34-36/ Mt:24:40/ Rev:3:10).

TWO PATHS: ONE DECISION

And now everyone who reads the words of this Book has a decision to make, for there are two paths you can walk down, a Path of Life and of Death.

PATH OF LIFE

Embrace The Truth of The Gospel, of who JESUS is *(The True SON & CLONE of GOD)*, and of Salvation and Prophecy as found in The Apostle's Creed and leave these Churches of hell and error. Follow JESUS' Teaching for real, pray and live The Lord's Prayer everyday, start your own Church of Philadelphia = "2 or 3" in your own home and COME OUT OF THESE DEAD CHURCHES AND BE YE SEPARATE.

This step in faith and Love for God (above) will put you on the path of Eternal Life and release the Power of God in your own life and home gathering. This will place you on the path of having your walk with God, "Accounted Worthy" to ESCAPE The Coming Tribulation, in the First of Two Raptures! OVERCOMING FEAR AND TEMPTATION IN YOUR OWN LIFE AND WALK WITH GOD. (Lu:21:34-36).

PATH OF DEATH

Stay in your dead, powerless Churches with their false Trinity and the multiplex of false doctrines and delusions about Salvation Prophecy and The Rapture = and find yourself LEFT BEHIND when JESUS comes for his true followers, his worthy believers, his Church of Philadelphia. For you allowed FEAR AND LOVE OF SIN TO BLIND,CORRUPT and OVERCOME YOUR MIND AND SOUL.

WARNING: when you embrace Satan's Lie of "Once Saved, Always Saved", (OSAS) you have already placed yourself upon the Path of Death, on the Baptist "Highway To Hell".

CHOOSE LIFE!!!

God Bless,
Pastor Harry/Church of Philadelphia-Internet@

www.SATANSRAPTURE.COM &

www.SATANSRAPTURE.ORG (mirror site).

BIOGRAHPHY/
ABOUT THE AUTHOR

have studied Bible Prophecy and Theology since 1982. I published my first book in 1986, THE ANSWER-TWO RAPTURES. I published my second book, on June 6 2006 entitled JUNE 6 2006 (666) ANTICHRIST REVEALED. In both instances, I solved, (with God's Help) Two Biblical Mysteries, 1) that of the "Rapture" of The Church and 2) the name and Identity of The Antichrist. On both subjects, the Churches and their leaders are very much mistaken.

I am uniquely qualified to write this book because I think "outside of the box" and I am not afraid to accept new concepts and ideas which go against the mainstream and the "norm". As to my personal life, it is just that, "personal". I live in NY State and plan to move west to a rural area before DEC 21 2012... PEACE.